WINFIELD AND JOLOWICZ ON TORT

EIGHTEENTH EDITION, 2010

BY

W. V. H. ROGERS, M.A.

of Gray's Inn, Barrister;
Senior Fellow in the University of Nottingham

SWEET & MAXWELL  THOMSON REUTERS

Preface

order to protect litigants
abusive claims."

So this is not a likely growt

(5) The HCA upheld the
(Ch.6) to reformulate the l
chance: see [2010] HCA 12
and notes) refers to the diff
in common law and some
apparent differences on this

The University of Notting
back after a long absence, h
as could be wished for over
and Stephen Todd, has pro
two amiable colleagues of
express my thanks to the e
assistance and efficiency. Th
back a long way and I canr

HORSFORTH
June, 2010.

---

quickly rack up alarming costs expenditure for both sides. A pa
ular area of controversy has been "libel tourism". Americans ar
diffident about promoting the merits of their own institution
rarely pay much regard to what happens outside their shores
respect, seeming to believe, as Lord Hoffmann said in his
Ebsworth Memorial Lecture, "the whole world should shar
view about how to strike the balance between freedom of exp
and the defence of reputation". It is not surprising that he go
deal of abuse for his views but what is disheartening (the
surprising) is that nowhere in the "serious newspaper" con
this issue would you have discovered that the supposedly a
law here on the reporting of matters of public concern
recent growth and is more or less the same everywhere
United States: Australia, New Zealand, Canada (at the er
and Ireland (by statute in 2009). But slogans are easier

No doubt there will be further important decisions
book is published but I would draw attention to the foll
which occurred or came to my attention after submiss
not be incorporated.

(1) The current complexity of limitation law has be
above. An illustration is *Williams v Lishman, Sidwel*
Price Ltd [2010] EWCA Civ 1418. D causes a loss
deliberately conceals for the purposes of s.32 of the
1980; there then occurs a second loss (arising from
of duty) which D does not conceal. Is the first los
to the plaintiff's right of action" so as to prevent
the facts it was held that both losses occurred sim
issue did not arise but Rix L.J. inclined to the view
hypothesis s.32 would operate in favour of th
are:

"[O]dd consequences whichever solution is
said that there is no logic or justice in allowir
concealed loss to extend the time for bring
claimant subsequently incurs a much large
acted sufficiently promptly with respect to
that, why should the existence of a small
claimant may well consider is not won
running against a claimant who only disco
suffered a far greater earlier loss that h
him?"

(Elias L.J.).

(2) In Ch.22, *Muuse v Secretary of St*
ment is cited as illustrating that exemplary
for misfeasance in a public office. The CA ([2010] EWCA

In the last few years I have become accus
Lords making some radical changes to tort law
year when this book had already been set up. I
six-and-a-half pages of a seven-and-a-half-pa
devoted to this phenomenon. Those late devel
v Corus and *Customs and Excise v Barclays Ba*
into this edition. This time, the schedule requir
Preface rather earlier. Whether or not the Supre
thing up its sleeve this Term, there are upcoming
wicz v Greif (UK) Ltd (proof of causation, Ch.6)
Scottish Power (breach of statutory duty, Ch.6)
Energy (damages for subterranean trespass, Ch.
lative front there is not a great deal of lawyer's l
years. It is now nine years since the Law Comm
cleansing of the Augean stables of limitation of ac
not appear even in the *draft* Civil Law Reform Bil
it had been promised. For that nine years of inactio
on crime, criminal justice, policing and terrorism
3,347 pages of the statute book.

This is a book about tort doctrine, the substantive l
in operation is the focus of the current crisis (not too
over costs and the financing of litigation, It may be
significant event since the last edition is the appearan
L.J.'s *Review of Civil Litigation Costs*. This monu
(produced with astonishing speed) appeared not long b
had to be submitted, but some of its principal recomm
outlined in the context of personal injuries in Ch.1. It
that the success fees and after the event insurance (ATI
associated with Conditional Fee Agreements should
recoverable by the successful claimant, since these ar
factors which have driven up costs over the last few year
just a matter of defendants' liability insurers having to pay
there has been litigation on a pretty heroic scale betv
insurers and claimants' solicitors who, the insurers alle
properly to vet the strength of claims brought with ATI
(*Axa Insurance v Akther & Derby*, Ch.26).

First Edition
Second Edition
Third Edition
Fourth Edition
Fifth Edition
Sixth Edition
Seventh Edition
Eighth Edition
Ninth Edition

Tenth Edition
Eleventh Edition
Twelfth Edition
Reprinted
Thirteenth Edition
Fourteenth Edition   (
Fifteenth Edition   (
Reprinted   (1
Reprinted   (2
Sixteenth Edition   (20
Reprinted   (20
Seventeenth Edition   (20
Eighteenth Edition   (201

        Published in 2010 by Th
        (Registered in England &
        Registered Office a
        100 Avenue Road, Lon
                    Sweet &
    For further information on o
            www.sweetan
        Typeset by Interactive S
                Printed in t
            CPI William Clowes

            A CIP catalog
        for this book i
            from the Britis.

    No natural forests were destroy
        only farmed timber was u

            ISBN 978–1847–

Thomson Reuters and the Thomson Reuters Log
Sweet & Maxwell® is a registered trademark o

    Crown Copyright material is reprodu
    of the Controller of HMSO and the Qu

                    ©
            Thomson Reuters
            (Legal) Limited
                2010

As far as the basic structure of the law is con
ment of the economic torts in *OBG v Allan* (C
most important development (though it is ironic
studying Torts nowadays will ever be exposed
Customs v Total on conspiracy ensures that we
"symmetrical" system but there is no doubt
progress in simplifying this area. In the last fe
trade disputes has tended to be about the deta
shall have to see how the statutory structure o
the "*Thomson v Deakin/Rookes v Barnard*"
OBG v Allan.

The Duty of Care War (now 40 years old
v Dorset Yacht Co as the first engagemen
little quieter than in the period covered by
relationship between tort law and publi
trouble. If the defendants' application fo
Connor v Surrey C.C. (Ch.5) is successf
have another opportunity to look at the is
has produced provisional proposals in th
in Ch.5, but they do not seem to hav
received.

Defamation continues to give troubl
the *Reynolds* principle in *Jameel v*
After submission of the text, the CA
ciation v Singh (briefly mentioned in
a statement that the defendants "h
ments" was capable of being read as
for which the defendant believed t
and hence fell within the scope of
case turns on its particular facts, f
about the difference between fact
ments" as the European Court of I
But that conceals a deeper proble
the newspaper in which the state
and, as Lord Judge C.J. put it
[had] been created that this [wa
one of its critics", the issue of
matter of very legitimate inter
been abandoned and the BCA
defendant will have suffered
litigation and will no doubt be
review of defamation law a
Lester's Defamation Bill (M
probably to inform the revie
fect, but like much else ir
substantive rules than the

reversed the
made out or
officials kne
(as opposed
upheld the a
native claim
(protected b
outrageous.
would not h
been made

(3) Credit
erty damage
v Hoyer Gr
(4) The
Securities P
W.L.R. 126
proceedings
mission to
offices. The
ton L.J. sai

"[E]ven
compulsi
there is
beyond th
invocatio
clusion v
earlier ca
House of
cution to
the cause
dient of
reasonabl
but to ex
process
good cau

Mummery

"[C]ourts
the cond
protect t
powers t
condition
of legal
ment pro

CONTENTS

	PAGE
Preface to Eighteenth Edition	v
Table of Cases	xiii
Table of Statutes	xci
Table of Statutory Instruments	ciii
Table of European Legislation	cv
Table of Abbreviations	cvii

CHAPTER

		PAGE
1.	Nature and Functions of the Law of Tort	1
2.	The Structure of Tort Law: History and Influences	59
3.	General Characteristics of Tortious Liability	87
4.	Trespass to the Person and Related Matters	97
5.	Negligence: Duty and Breach	149
6.	Negligence: Causation, Remoteness (Scope of Liability) and Contributory Negligence	305
7.	Breach of Statutory Duty and Misfeasance in a Public Office	383
8.	Employers' Liability	411
9.	Liability for Land and Structures	439
10.	Liability for Defective Products	487
11.	Liability for Statements	521
12.	Defamation, Privacy and Related Matters	567
13.	Trespass to Land	685
14.	Nuisance	705
15.	Strict Liability: Rule in Rylands v Fletcher	763
16.	Animals	799
17.	Interference with Goods	817
18.	Interference with Contract or Business	859
19.	Abuse of Legal Procedure	923
20.	Vicarious Liability	943
21.	Joint and Several Tortfeasors	987
22.	Remedies	1005
23.	Death in Relation to Tort	1079
24.	Capacity	1097

TABLE OF CASES

384238 Ontario Ltd v R (1984) 8 D.L.R. (4th) 676 17–8
4Eng Ltd v Harper [2008] EWHC 915 11–14
671122 Ontario Ltd v Sagaz Industries Canada Ltd [2001] SCC 59 20–5
24 Seven Utility Services Ltd v Rosekey Ltd, February 18, 2004 (QB) 26–28
A (Children) (Conjoined Twins: Surgical Separation), Re [2001] Fam. 147 .... 4–8, 4–11,
                                                                                        25–35
A v B [2007] EWHC 1246 (QB) 11–1
A v Bottrill [2002] UKPC 44; [2003] 1 A.C. 449 .... 1–40, 22–12
A v Essex CC [2003] EWCA Civ 1848; [2004] 1 W.L.R. 1881 .... 5–50, 5–51, 5–53
A v Hoare [2005] EWHC 2161 (QB) 4–3, 26–18, 26–19
A v MoD [2004] EWCA Civ 641; [2005] Q.B. 183 .... 8–17, 20–6
A v National Blood Authority [2001] 3 All E.R. 289 .. 6–6, 10–16, 10–19, 10–20, 10–21,
                                                              10–23, 22–19, 22–37, 22–38
A v New South Wales [2007] HCA 10 .... 19–7, 19–8
A v Tameside and Glossop HA (1996) 35 B.M.L.R. 77 .... 5–73, 5–76
A v UK (2003) E.H.R.R. 51 12–39
A, Re [2001] Fam. 147 24–14
A & W Hemphill Ltd v Williams 1966 S.C.(H.L.) 31 20–10
A C Billings & Sons Ltd v Riden [1958] A.C. 240 .... 3–6, 6–48
AB v Ministry of Defence [2009] EWHC 1225 (QB) 26–7, 26–18
AB v Nugent Care Society [2009] EWCA Civ 827 26–21
AB v South West Water Services Ltd [1993] Q.B. 507 .... 22–8, 22–10, 22–11
ABC v O'Neill [2006] HCA 46 12–86
AD v Bury MBC [2006] EWCA Civ 1 5–53
AD v East Kent Community NHS Trust [2002] EWCA Civ 1872; [2003] 3 All E.R.
    1167 24–15
AH v AB [2009] EWCA Civ 1092 .... 19–3, 19–4
AIC Ltd v ITS Testing Services (UK) Ltd [2006 EWCA Civ 1601; [2007] 1 Lloyd's
    Rep 555 .... 11–10, 11–13, 26–4
AMF International Ltd v Magnet Bowling Ltd [1968] 1 W.L.R. 1028 ...... 9–4, 9–15, 9–16,
                                                                            9–24, 9–30
AMP General Insurance Ltd v Roads and Traffic Authority of NSW [2001] NSWCA
    186 6–41
AT v Dulghieru [2009] EWHC 225 (QB) 22–10
Abbahall Ltd v Smee [2002] EWCA Civ 1831; [2003] 1 W.L.R. 1472 22–47
Abbott v Refuge Assurance Co Ltd [1962] 1 Q.B. 432 .... 19–5, 19–8, 19–9
Abbott v Will Gannon & Smith Ltd [2005] EWCA Civ 198; [2005] P.N.L.R. 30 26–12
Abraham v G. Ireson & Son (Properties) Ltd [2009] EWHC 1958 (QB) 8–5
Abrahams v Deaking [1891] 1 Q.B. 516 20–11
Abrath v North Eastern Ry (1886) 11 App. Cas. 247 .... 19–7, 19–11
Abu Dhabi Investment Co v H. Clarkson & Co [2008] EWCA Civ 699 11–11
Ackland v Commonwealth [2007] NSWCA 250 6–46
Acton v Blundell (1843) 12 M. & W. 324 14–12
Adam v Ward [1917] A.C. 309 .... 12–38, 12–46, 12–51, 12–64

Adams (Durham) Ltd v Trust Houses Ltd [1960] 1 Lloyd's Rep. [1970] 1 Q.B. 177 20–15
Adams v Bracknell Forest BC [2004] UKHL 29; [2005] 1 A.C. 76 ... 26–18, 26–19, 26–21
Adams v Guardian Newspapers Ltd [2003] ScotCS 131; 2003 S.L.T. 1058 12–39
Adams v L & Y Ry (1869) L.R. 4 C.P. 739 6–49
Adams v Naylor [1946] A.C. 543 24–2
Adams v Rhymney Valley DC [2000] Lloyd's Rep. P.N. 777 5–81
Adams v Ursell [1913] 1 Ch. 269 14–30
Adamson v Jarvis (1827) 4 Bing. 66 21–4
Adamson v Motor Vehicle Insurance Trust (1957) 58 W.A.L.R. 56 24–26
Addis v Crocker [1961] 1 Q.B. 11 12–41
Adeels Palace Pty Ltd v Moubarak [2009] HCA 48 6–7
Adeels Palace Pty Ltd v Scott [2009] HCA 48 5–31
Ad-Lib Club Ltd v Granville [1972] R.P.C. 673 18–50
Admiralty Commissioners v SS Amerika [1917] A.C. 38 23–8
Admiralty Commissioners v SS Chekiang [1926] A.C. 637 .... 22–14, 22–43
Admiralty Commissioners v SS Susquehanna [1926] A.C. 655 .... 22–22, 22–40, 22–43
Admiralty Commissioners v SS Valeria [1922] 2 A.C. 242 22–16
Admiralty Commissioners v SS Volute [1922] 1 A.C. 129 6–49
Adset v West [1983] Q.B. 826 23–5
Advance Magazine Publishing v Redmond Publishing [1997] F.S.R. 449 18–45
Advanced Industrial Technology Corp. Ltd v Bond Street Jewellers Ltd [2006] EWCA
    Civ 923 11–4
Adventure Films Ltd v Tully, *The Times*, October 14, 1982 17–15
Aer Lingus v Gildacroft Ltd [2006] EWCA Civ 4 26–25
Aerospace Publishing Ltd v Thames Water Utilities Ltd [2005] EWHC 2987 22–44
Affutu-Nartey v Clarke, The Times, February 9, 1984 25–13
Ahmed v Shafique [2009] EWHC 618 (QB) 4–32
Aiken v Stewart Wrightson Members Agency Ltd [1995] 1 W.L.R. 1281 ... 5–22, 20–1, 20–22
Aikens v Wisconsin 195 U.S. 194 (1904) 1–15
Airedale NHS Trust v Bland [1993] A.C. 789 .... 4–8, 22–20
Airey v Ireland (1979) 2 E.H.R.R. 305 2–10
Airwork (NZ) Ltd v Vertical Flight Management Ltd [1999] 1 N.Z.L.R. 641, NZCA ... 20–8
Aitchison v Page Motors Ltd (1935) 154 L.T. 128 20–16
Aitken v Preston [1997] E.M.L.R. 415 12–70
Aitken v Richardson [1967] 2 N.Z.L.R. 15 17–8
Ajinomoto Sweeteners Europe SAS v Asda Stores Ltd [2009] EWHC 1717 (QB) ... 12–13
Akenzua v Secretary of State for the Home Dept [2002] EWCA Civ 1470; [2003] 1
    W.L.R. 54 .... 7–20, 7–23
Akerhielm v De Mare [1959] A.C. 789 11–13
Al Amoudi v Brisard [2006] EWHC 1062 12–22
Al Fagih v H H Saudi Research & Marketing (UK) Ltd [2001] EWCA Civ 1634;
    [2002] E.M.L.R. 13 12–27
Al Kandari v J R Brown & Co [1988] Q.B. 665 .... 5–59, 5–73
Al Nakib Investments (Jersey) Ltd v Longcroft [1990] 1 W.L.R. 1390 11–26
Al Raschid v News Syndicate Co, 191 N.E. 713 (1934) 12–73
Al Saudi Banque v Clarke Pixley [1990] Ch. 313 11–25
Al-Adsani v UK (2002) 34 E.H.R.R. 273 24–6
Albazero, The [1977] A.C. 774 .... 5–41, 22–16
Albert v Lavin [1982] A.C. 546 4–26
Albery and Budden v BP Oil [1980] J.P.L. 586 .... 5–82, 10–25
Albonetti v Wirral MBC [2008] EWCA Civ 783 26–18
Alcoa Minerals v Broderick [2002] 1 A.C. 371 22–44
Alcock v CC South Yorkshire [1992] 1 A.C. 310 ...... 5–61, 5–62, 5–63, 5–66, 5–68, 5–69,
                                                                                        5–70, 5–72, 5–74
Alcott v Miller's Karri etc. Ltd (1940) 91 L.T. 722 12–73
Aldred v Nacano [1987] I.R.L.R. 292 .... 8–11, 20–12
Aldred's Case (1610) 9 Co. 57b 16–2
Alexander v Rayson [1936] 1 K.B. 169 5–90
Alexander v Rolls Royce [1996] R.T.R. 95 22–43
Alexander v Ry Executive [1951] 2 K.B. 882 17–17
Alexander v Southey (1821) 5 B. & Ald.247 17–12

Design Services Ltd v Canada [2008] SCC 22 ....
Designers Guild Ltd v Russell Williams (Textiles) Ltd [2
Desmond v CC Nottinghamshire [2009] EWHC 2362 (Q
Despina R, The [1979] A.C. 685 ....
Devenish Nutrition Ltd v Sanofi-Aventis SA [2007] EWH
Devillez v Boots Pure Drug Co [1962] C.L.Y. 2015 ....
Dewey v White (1827) M. & M. 56 ....
Dews v NCB [1988] A.C. 1 ....
Deyong v Shenburn [1946] K.B. 227 ....
Dhesi v CC West Midlands, *The Times*, May 9, 2000, CA
Diamond v Bank of London & Montreal [1979] Q.B. 333
Dickenson v Watson (1681) T. Jones 205 ....
Dickins v O2 plc [2008] EWCA Civ 1144 ....
Didow v Alberta Power [1988] 5 W.W.R. 606 ....
Die Spoorbond v South African Railways [1956] A.C. 99
Dietz v Lennig Chemicals Ltd [1969] 1 A.C. 170 ....
Dillon v Twin State Gas and Electric Co, 163 A. 111 (N.
Dimbleby & Sons Ltd v NUJ [1984] 1 W.L.R. 427 ....
Dimond v Lovell [2002] 1 A.C. 384 ....
Dimskal Shipping Co SA v ITWF [1992] 2 A.C. 152 ......
DPP v Jones [1999] A.C. 240 ....
DPP v K (1990) 1 W.L.R. 1067 ....
Disley v Levine [2001] EWCA Civ 1087 ....
Dixon v Clement Jones Solicitors [2004] EWCA Civ 100
Dixon v Metropolitan Board of Works (1881) 7 Q.B.d. 41
Dobbie v Medway HA [1994] 1 W.L.R. 1234 ....
Dobell v Stevens (1825) 3 B. & C. 623 ....
Dobson v Dobson [1999] 2 S.C.R. 753 ....
Dobson v N Tyneside HA [1997] 1 W.L.R. 596 ....
Dobson v Thames Water [2009] EWCA Civ 28 ....
Dockrell v Douglas (1899) 80 L.T. 556 ....
Dodd Properties Ltd v Canterbury CC [1979] 2 All E.R. 1
Dodd Properties Ltd v Canterbury CC [1980] 1 W.L.R. 43
Dodds v Dodds [1978] Q.B. 543 ....
Dodkins v West Ham Utd [2000] C.L.Y. 4226 ....
Dodwell v Burford (1670) 1 Mod. 24 ....
Doe d Murray v Bridges (1831) 1 B. & Ad. 847 ....
Doe d v Bennett [2004] SCC17 ....
Doherty v Birmingham CC [2008] UKHL 57 ....
Dolbey v Goodwin [1955] 1 W.L.R. 553 ....
Doleman v Deakin, The Times, January 30, 1990 ....
Dollman v Hillman Ltd [1941] 1 All E.R. 355 ....
Dominion Mosaic & Tile Co Ltd v Trafalgar Trucking Co

Donachie v CC Greater Manchester [2004] EWCA Civ 40
Donaghey v Boulton & Paul Ltd [1968] A.C. 1 ....
Donaldson v MvNiven (1852) 96 S.J. 747 ....
Donnelly v Joyce [1974] Q.B. 454 ....
Donoghue v Folkestone Properties Ltd [2003] EWCA Civ
Donoghue v Hayes (1831) Hayes (Ir. Ex.) R. 265 ....
Donoghue v Stevenson [1932] A.C. 502 ... 1–3, 1–8, 5–3,
                                    5–16, 5–21, 5–37, 5–39, 5–4
                                    10–6, 10–8, 10–9, 10–1
Donovan v Cammell Laird & Co [1949] 2 All E.R. 82 .....
Donovan v Gwentoys Ltd [1990] 1 W.L.R. 472 ....
Dodeward v Spence (1908) 6 C.L.R. 406 ....
Dooley v Cammell Laird & Co Ltd [1951] 1 Lloyd's Rep.2
Dorman Long (Steel) Ltd v Bell [1964] 1 W.L.R. 333 ....
Dorta Ekenaike v Victoria Legal Aid [2005] HCA 12 .....
Doughty v Turner Manufacturing Co Ltd [1964] 1 Q.B. 518

Alexandrou v Oxford [1993] 4 All E.R. 328 5–27
Alexis v Newham LBC [2009] EWHC 1323 (QB) 5–85, 6–38
Alfred McAlpine Construction Ltd v Panatown Ltd [2001] 1 A.C. 518 9–32
Alghussein v Eton College [1988] 1 W.L.R. 587 11–32
Ali Reza-Delta Transport Co Ltd v United Arab Shipping Co SAG [2003] EWCA Civ
    684; [2003] 2 Lloyd's Rep. 450 22–41
Ali v Birmingham CC [2010] UKSC 8; [2010] 2 W.L.R. 471 7–5
Ali v Furness [1988] 2 Lloyd's Rep.1 5–79
Ali v Sydney Mitchell & Co [1980] A.C. 198 5–60
Alicia Hosiery Ltd v Brown Shipley & Co Ltd [1970] 1 Q.B. 195 13–3
Alker v Collingwood Housing Association [2007] EWCA Civ 343 9–40
Allan v Ellis & Co [1990] 11 E.G. 78 11–14
Allan v Liverpool Overseers (1874) L.R. 9 Q.B. 180 13–2
Allan v New Mount Sinai Hospital (1980) 109 D.L.R. (3d) 643 3–2
Allason v BBC Worldwide, *The Times*, January 24, 1998 12–71
Allbutt v General Council of Medical Education (1889) 23 Q.B.D. 400 12–53
Allen v BREL Ltd [2001] EWCA Civ 242; [2001] I.C.R. 942 21–1
Allen v Flood [1898] A.C. 1 .... 3–9, 14–12, 18–3, 18–11
Allen v Gulf Oil Refining Ltd [1981] A.C. 1001 14–34
Allen v Southwark LBC [2008] EWCA Civ 1478 4–38
Allied Finance & Investments Ltd v Haddow [1983] N.Z.L.R. 22 11–22
Allied Maples Group Ltd v Simmons & Simmons [1995] 1 W.L.R. 1602 6–15
Allin v City & Hackney HA (1996) 7 Med.L.R. 91 5–73
Allison v London Underground Ltd [2008] EWCA Civ 71; [2008] I.C.R. 719 ..... 3–5, 8–6
Allsop v Allsop (1865) 5 H. & N. 534 12–5
Almeda v Att-Gen for Gibraltar [2003] UKPC 81 2–13
Alnwick, The [1965] P. 357 26–22
Aloe Coal Co v Clark Equipment Co 816, R. 2d 110 10–10
Al-Rawas v Pegasus Energy Ltd [2008] EWHC 617 22–10
Amaca Pty Ltd v Ellis [2010] HCA 5 6–7
Amalgamated Metal Trading Ltd v DTI, *The Times*, March 21, 1989 11–3
Amalgamated Televison Services Pty Ltd v Marsden (1998) 43 N.S.W.L.R. 158 12–14
American Cyanamid Ltd v Ethicon Ltd [1975] A.C. 396 .... 18–43, 18–52, 22–50
American Express Co v British Airways Board [1983] 1 W.L.R. 701 ...... 1–12, 7–3, 17–18
Anchor Brewhouse Developments v Berkley House (Docklands Developments)
    (1987) 284 E.G. 625 .... 13–7, 22–48, 22–53
Anchor Products Ltd v Hedges (1966) 115 C.L.R. 493 5–89
Ancona v Rogers (1876) L.R. 1 Ex. D. 285 17–5
Anderson Group Pty Ltd v Tynan Motors Pty Ltd [2006] NSWCA 22 17–18
Anderson v Christian Salvesen plc [2006] CSOH 101; 2006 S.L.T. 815 5–69
Anderson v Coutts (1894) 58 J.P. 369 9–6
Anderson v Earlanger [1980] C.L.Y. 133 17–10
Anderson v Lyotier [2008] EWHC 2790 (QB) 6–47
Anderson v Minneapolis etc Ry, 179 N.W. 45 (Minn 1920) 6–7
Anderson v New York Telephone Co, 361 N.Y.S. 2d 913 (1974) 12–23
Anderson v Newham F.E. College [2002[EWCA Civ 505 6–53
Anderson v Oppenheimer (1880) L.R. 5 Q.B.D. 602 15–14
Andreae v Selfridge & Co [1938] Ch. 11 .... 14–7, 14–11
Andrew v Kounis Freeman [1999] 2 B.C.L.C. 641 11–27
Andrew Weir Shipping Ltd v Wartsila UK Ltd [2004] EWHC 1284 (Comm); [2004]
    2 Lloyd's Rep. 377 .... 10–10, 11–23
Andrews v Freeborough [1967] 1 Q.B. 1 22–19
Andrews v Grand & Toy Alberta Ltd (1978) 83 D.L.R. (3d) 452 22–16
Andrews v Hopkinson [1957] 1 Q.B. 229 .... 9–36, 10–5, , 11–6
Andrews v Initial Cleaning Services Ltd [2000] I.C.R. 166 .... 8–13, 21–6
Andrews v Mockford [1896] 1 Q.B. 372 11–11
Andrews v Reading BC [2005] EWHC 256 (QB) 14–22
Andrews v Schooling [1991] 1 W.L.R. 783 9–38
Aneco Reinsurance Underwriting Ltd v Johns & Higgs Ltd [2001] UKHL 51; [2002]
    1 Lloyd's Rep. 157 6–28
Angell v H H Bushell & Co Ltd [1968] 1 Q.B. 813 12–11

Davie v New Merton Board Mills
Davies v Davies [1975] Q.B. 172
Davies v Marshall (1861) 10 C.B.(
Davies v Presbyterian Church [198
Davies v Solomon (1871) L.R. 7 Q
Davies v Swan Motor Co [1949] 2
Davies v Taylor [1974] A.C. 207 ..
Davies v Whiteways Cyder Co Ltd
Davies and Davies v Smith and Sm
Davis v Lisle [1936] 2 K.B. 434 ...
Davis v New England College at A
Davis v St Mary's Demolition & E
Davis v Stena Line Ltd [2005] EW
Davy-Chieseman v Davy-Chiesman
Dawkins v Lord Paulet (1869) L.R.
Dawkins v Lord Rokeby (1875) L.F
Dawnay Day & Co Ltd v Cantor Fi
Dawson & Co v Bingley UDC [191
Dawson Bloodstock Agency v Mirr
Dawson v CC Northumbria [2009] I
Day v Brownrigg (1878) 10 Ch.D. 2
De Sales v Ingrilli [2002] HCA 52,
Dean v Allin & Watts [2001] EWCA

Dean v Hogg (1834) 10 Bing. 345 ..
Deane v Clayton (1817) 7 Taunt. 48
Deatons Pty Ltd v Flew (1949) 79 C
De Beers Products Ltd v Internation
    W.L.R. 972 ....
De Buse v McCarthy [1942] 1 K.B.
Deep Vein Thrombosis and Air Trave
    3 W.L.R. 1320 ....
De Francesco v Barnum (1890) 45 C
De Franco v MPC, *The Times*, May 8
Dehn v Att-Gen [1988] 2 N.Z.L.R. 5
De Hoghton v Money (1866) L.R. 2
De Jetley Marks v Greenwood [1936]
De Keyser's Royal Hotel Ltd v Spice
De La Bere v Pearson [1908] 1 K.B.
Delaney v T P Smith Ltd [1946] K.B
Delaware Mansions Ltd v Westminste

Dellabarca v Storeman and Packers U
Deloitte Haskins & Sells v National N
Delta Holdings Ltd v Magrum (1975)
Dempsey v Waterford Corp [2008] IE
Denham v Midland Employers Mutua
Dennis v Charnwood BC [1983] Q.B.
Dennis v MoD [2003] EWHC 793, QB;

Department of Education v Thomas B
De Parell v Walker (1932) 49 T.L.R. 3
Dept of Natural Resources v Harper [2
Dept of Transport v NW Water Author
Dept of Transport v NW Water Author
Derbyshire CC v Times Newspapers L
Derbyshire CC v Times Newspapers L
Dering v Uris [1964] 2 Q.B. 669 ....
Derry v Peek (1889) 14 App. Cas. 337
Design Properties Ltd v Thurloe Proper
    C.R. 594 ....

Esso Petroleum Co Ltd v Mardon [1976] Q.B. 801 .... 11–18, 11–21
Esso Petroleum Co Ltd v Southport Corp [1956] A.C. 218 .... 2–2, 14–1, 25–33
Esterhuizen v Allied Dunbar Assurance Plc [1998] 2 F.L.R. 668 5–59
Ettingshausen v Australian Consolidated Press (1991) 23 N.S.W.L.R. 443 12–79
European Commission v UK [1997] All E.R. (E.C.) 481 10–23
Evans v Kosmar Villa Holidays plc [2007] EWCA Civ 1003; [2008] 1 W.L.R. 297 9–17
Evans v London Hospital Medical College [1981] 1 W.L.R. 184 .... 5–60, 12–41
Evans v Triplex Safety Glass Co [1936] 1 All E.R. 283 .... 10–1, 10–7
Everett v Ribbands [1952] 2 Q.B. 198 19–6
Everitt v Martin [1953] N.Z.L.R. 29 .... 14–38, 17–3
Exel Logistics Ltd v Curran [2004] EWCA Civ 1249 7–9
Express and Echo Publications Ltd v Tanton [1999] I.R.L.R. 367 20–5
Express and Star Newspapers v NGA (1982) [1985] I.R.L.R. 455 18–35
Express Newspapers Ltd v McShane [1980] A.C. 672 18–37
F (in utero), Re [1988] Fam. 122 4–8
F v West Berkshire HA [1990] 2 A.C. 1 4–7
F v Wirral MBC [1991] Fam. 69 .... 11–14, 18–1, 18–8
FFSB Ltd v Seward & Kissel LLP [2007] UKPC 16 21–6
Fabri v Morris [1947] 1 All E.R. 315 14–39
Fagan v Goodman, unreported, November 30, 2001 (QB) 5–63
Fagan v MPC [1969] 1 A.B. 439 4–6
Fairchild v Glenhaven Funeral Services Ltd [2002] UKHL 22; [2003] 1 A.C. 32 .... 2–17, 6–9,
                                          6–10, 6–11, 6–13, 9–2, 9–3, 9–16, 21–1
Fairclaim v Shamtitle (1762) 3 Burr. 1290 13–15
Fairline Shipping Corp v Adamson [1975] Q.B. 180 .... 9–24, 17–11, 24–23
Faleigh v Goschen [1898] 1 Ch. 73 24–2
Fallas v Mourlas [2006] NSWCA 32 25–11
Fangrove Pty Ltd v Tod Group Holdings Pty Ltd [1999] 2 Qd R 236 9–36
Farah v British Airways, *The Times*, January 26, 2000, CA 2–5, 11–35
Farah v MPC [1998] Q.B. 65 .... 2–18, 20–7
Fardon v Harcourt-Rivington (1932) 146 L.T. 391 .... 5–83, 16–2, 25–27
Farley v Skinner [2001] UKHL 49 .... 5–62, 5–72
Farmer Giles v Wessex Water [1990] E.G. 102 22–44
Farmer v Hunt (1610) 1 Brownl. 220 17–3
Farmer v Hyde [1937] 1 K.B. 728 12–44
Farnworth v Manchester Corp [1929] 1 K.B. 533 25–38
Farraj v Kings Healthcare NHS Trust [2009] EWCA Civ 1203 20–6
Farrant v Thompson (1822) 5 B. & Ald. 826 17–8
Farrell v John Mowlem & Co Ltd [1954] 1 Lloyd's Rep. 437 14–39
Farrer v Nelson (1885) 15 Q.B.D. 258 16–2
Farrington v Leigh, *The Times*, December 10, 1987 12–21
Farrugia v GW Ry [1947] 2 All E.R. 565 13–5
Fashion Brokers Ltd v Clarke Hayes [2000] Lloyd's Rep. P.N. 398 11–20
Faulkner v Willetts [1982] R.T.R. 159 9–6
Fawcett Security Operations (Pvt) Ltd v Omar Enterprises (Pvt) Ltd [1991] 2
    S.A.L.R. 20–15
Fawcett v Smethurst (1915) 84 L.J.K.B. 473 24–17
Fay v Prentice (1845) 1 C.B. 828 14–28
Fayed v Al-Tajir [1988] Q.B. 712 12–43
Fayed v MPC [2004] EWCA Civ 1579 .... 4–23, 4–24
Fellows v Fisher [1976] Q.B. 122 22–50
Femis-Bank (Anguilla) Ltd v Lazar [1991] Ch. 391 22–50
Fenn v Peterborough CC (1976) 73 D.L.R. (3d) 177 5–67
Fennell v Robson Excavations Pty Ltd [1977] 2 N.S.W.L.R. 486 14–17
Fennelly v Connex South Eastern [2001] I.R.L.R. 390 20–14
Fennings v Grenville (1808) 1 Taunt. 241 17–15
Ferguson v British Gas Trading Ltd [2009] EWCA Civ 46; [2010] 1 W.L.R. 785 4–38
Ferguson v John Dawson & Partners (Contractors) Ltd [1976] 1 W.L.R. 1213 20–3
Ferguson v Welsh [1987] 1 W.L.R. 1553 .... 9–6, 9–8, 9–14, 9–16, 9–22, 20–12
Fetter v Beale (1701) 1 Ld.Raym. 339 22–2
Fiala v Cechmanek (2001) 201 D.L.R. (4th) 680 24–26

Fielding v Variety Inc [1967] 2 Q.B. 841 12–75
Filliter v Phippard (1847) 11 Q.B. 347 15–21
Fine Art Society v Union Bank of London (1886) 17 Q.B.D. 705 17–8
Fine Cotton Spinners v Cash (1907) 24 R.P.C. 533 18–46
Finnis v Caulfield [2002] EWHC 3223 (QB) 25–22
Firma C-Trade SA v Newcastle Protection & Indemnity Asociation [1991] 2 A.C. 1 26–31
Firman v Ellis [1978] Q.B. 886 .... 26–20, 26–21
First Energy (UK) Ltd v Hungarian International Bank Ltd [1993] 2 Lloyd's Rep.
    194 20–17
Firth v Bowling Iron Co (1878) 3 C.P.D. 254 15–6
Fischer (George) GB Ltd v Multi-Construction Ltd [1995] 1 B.C.L.C. 260 24–21
Fishenden v Higgs & Hill Ltd (1935) 152 L.T. 128 22–53
Fisher v CHT Ltd (No 2) 9–4
Fisher v Harrods [1966] 1 Lloyd's Rep. 500 .... 10–1, 10–4
Fisher v Oldham Corp [1930] 2 K.B. 364 20–7
Fisher v Prince (1762) 3 Burr. 1363 .... 17–8, 17–29
Fitter v Veal (1701) 12 Mod. 542 22–2
Fitzgerald v AD and ED Cooke Bourne Farms Ltd [1964] 1 Q.B. 249 16–7
Fitzgerald v Lane [1989] A.C. 328 .... 6–42, 6–55, 21–1, 21–6
Fitzjohn v Mackinder (1861) 9 C.B. (N.S.) 505 19–3
Fitzsimmons v Ford Motor Co [1946] 1 All E.R. 429 8–10
Flack v Hudson [2001] Q.B. 698 16–5
Flannery v Halifax Estate Agencies Ltd [2000] 1 W.L.R. 377 5–79
Fleming v Securities Commission [1995] 2 N.Z.L.R. 514 5–31
Fletcher v Autocar and Transporters Ltd [1968] 2 Q.B. 322 22–19
Fletcher v Commissioners of Public Works [2003] 1 I.R. 465 .... 5–64, 22–19
Fletcher v National Mutual Life Nominee Ltd [1990] 1 N.Z.L.R. 97 21–7
Fletcher v Rylands (1866) L.R. 1 Ex. 265 .... 14–34, 14–38, 20–24, 25–27
Flood v Times Newspapers Ltd [2009] EWHC 2375 (QB) 12–53, 12–54
Flower v Ebbw Vale Steel, Iron and Coal Co Ltd [1934] 2 K.B. 132 6–52
Fogarty v UK (2002) 34 E.H.R.R. 12 2–13
Fontaine v British Columbia [1998] 1 S.C.R. 424 5–89
Fookes v Slaytor [1978] 1 W.L.R. 1293 6–43
Forbes v Wandsworth HA [1997] Q.B. 402 26–19
Ford v Foster (1872) L.R. 7 Ch. 611 18–46
Ford v Liverpool Corp (1973) 117 S.J. 167 14–44
Forest v Sharp (1963) 107 S.J. 536 22–19
Forrester v Tyrell (1893) 9 T.L.R. 257 12–4
Forsikringsaktieselskapet Vesta v Butcher [1988] 3 W.L.R. 565 6–44
Forster v Outred & Co 1982] 1 W.L.R. 86 26–10
Forsyth-Grant v Allen [2008] EWCA Civ 505 22–13
Fortnum & Mason Plc v Fortnam Ltd [1994] F.S.R. 438 18–48
Forward v Pittard (1785) 1 T.R. 27 15–17
Fosbroke-Hobbes v Airwork Ltd [1937] 1 All E.R. 108 9–22
Foskett v McKeown [2001] 1 A.C. 102 17–11
Foskett v Mistry [1984] R.T.R. 1 5–83
Foss v Fedden (1872) L.R. 7 Q.B. 661 15–13
Foster v British Gas Plc [1991] 2 A.C. 306 8–8
Foster v Warblington UDC [1906] 1 K.B. 648 14–15
Fouldes v Willoughby (1841) 8 M. & W. 538 .... 17–3, 17–8
Fountain v Boodle (1842) 3 Q.B. 5 12–64
Fowler v Jones, unreported, June 10, 2002 14–1
Fowler v Lanning [1959] 1 Q.B. 426 .... 4–33, 4–34, 13–1, 17–3
Fowles v Bedfordshire CC [1995] P.I.Q.R. P380 .... 5–30, 9–3
Fox, Campbell and Hartley v UK (1990) 13 E.H.R.R. 157 4–29
Foxcroft v Lacey (1613) Hob. 8917 12–21
France v Gaudet (1871) L.R. 6 Q.B. 199 17–27
France v Parkinson [1954] 1 W.L.R. 581 6–51
France, Fenwick & Co Ltd v R [1927] 1 K.B. 52 24–2
Francovich v Italy (C–6/90) [1995] I.C.R. 722 5–55
Francovich v Italy [1995] I.C.R. 722 .... 7–12, 8–8

HIH Casualty and General Insurance Ltd v Chase Manhattan Bank [2003] UKHL 6;
[2003] 2 Lloyd's Rep. 61 11–30
H N Emanuel Ltd v GLC [1971] 2 All E.R. 835 .... 15–20, 20–25
H West & Son Ltd v Shephard [1964] A.C. 326 .... 22–16, 22–19, 22–20, 22–21
Habib Bank v Habib Bank AG Zurich [1981] 1 W.L.R. 1265 18–46
Hackshaw v Shaw (1984) 155 C.L.R. 614 4–35
Haddow v Secretary of State for the Environment [2000] Env L.R. 212 11–20
Hadmor Productions Ltd v Hamilton [1983] 1 A.C. 191 .... 18–38, 18–40
Hagen v ICI [2002] I.R.L.R. 31 .... 11–12, 11–21
Hahn v Conley (1971) 126 C.L.R. 378 5–29
Haigh v Royal Steam Packet Co Ltd (1883) 52 L.J.Q.B. 640 23–11
Haines v Florensa (1990) 8 E.G. 7 13–7
Hale v Jennings Bros [1938] 1 All E.R. 579 .... 15–6, 15–9
Haley v London Electricity Board [1965] A.C. 778 .... 5–22, 5–84, 5–86, 6–48
Halford v Brooks [1991] 1 W.L.R. 428 1–2
Halford v UK (1997) 24 E.H.R.R. 523 2–8
Hall v Barclay [1937] 3 All E.R. 620 17–27
Hall v Brooklands Auto Racing Club [1933] 1 K.B. 205 3–6
Hall v Duke of Norfolk [1900] 2 Ch. 165 14–23
Hall v Gwent Healthcare NHS Trust [2005] EWCA Civ 919 .... 4–37, 5–71
Hall v Hebert [1993] 2 S.C.R. 159 .... 25–20, 25–21
Hall v Holker Estate Co Ltd [2008] EWCA Civ 1422 5–90
Hall v Lorimer 1992 S.T.C. 599 20–4
Hall v Woolston Hall Leisure Ltd [2001] 1 W.L.R. 225 25–22
Halsey v Esso Petroleum Co Ltd [1961] 1 W.L.R. 683 .... 14–1, 14–7
Hamble Fisheries Ltd v Gardner [1999] 2 Lloyd's Rep. 1 .... 10–3, 11–8, 11–23
Hambley v Shepley (1967) 63 D.L.R. (2d) 94 25–12
Hambley v Trott (1776) 1 Cowp. 371 25–36
Hamilton Jones v David & Snape [2003] EWHC 3147; [2004] 1 W.L.R. 924 18–1
Hamilton v Al-Fayed [2001] A.C. 395 .... 12–39, 19–15
Hamilton v Clifford [2004] EWCA Civ 1407 12–33
Hamilton v Papakura DC [2000] 1 N.Z.L.R. 265 .... 14–14, 15–3
Hamps v Darby [1948] 2 K.B. 311 16–14
Hampstead Heath Winter Swimming Club v London Corp [2005] EWHC 713
(Admin); [2005] 1 W.L.R. 2930 .... 1–45, 9–17
Hampton v Minns [2001] 1 W.L.R. 21–5
Hanbury v Hanbury (1892) 8 T.L.R. 559 24–26
Hancock v BW Brazier (Anerley) Ltd [1966] 1 W.L.R. 1317 .... 9–32, 9–38
Handcock v Baker (1800) 2 Bos. & P. 260 13–11
Hankinson v Bilby (1847) 16 M. & W. 422 12–16
Hannah v Peel [1945] K.B. 509 17–21
Hanrahan v Ainsworth (1990) 22 N.S.W.L.R. 73 19–14
Hanson v Bloom Camillin (No.2) [2000] Lloyd's Rep. P.N. 89 6–15
Hanson v Waller [1901] 1 Q.B. 390 20–11
Harbutt's "Plasticine" Ltd v Wayne Tank & Pump Co Ltd [1907] 1 Q.B. 447 .... 22–44, 22–45
Hardaker v Idle D C [1896] 1 Q.B. 335 .... 20–21, 20–24, 20–27
Hardie & Lane Ltd v Chilton [1928] 2 K.B. 306 3–6
Hardwick v Hudson [1999] 1 W.L.R. 1770 22–37
Hargreave v Goldman (1963) 37 A.L.J.R. 277 14–4
Hargreaves v Bretherton [1959] 1 Q.B. 45 .... 19–14, 24–10
Harnett v Bond [1925] A.C 669 6–36
Harper v Charlesworth (1825) 4 B. & C. 574 13–16
Harper v Haden & Sons Ltd [1933] Ch. 298 14–38
Harrhy v Thames Trains Ltd [2003] EWHC 2286 (QB) 5–69
Harris v Birkenhead Corp [1976] 1 W.L.R. 279 .... 9–4, 9–25
Harris v Brights Asphalt Contractors [1953] 1 Q.B. 617 .... 8–10, 22–36
Harris v Digital Pulse Pty Ltd [2003] N.S.W.C.A. 10, 44 A.C.S.R. 390 22–12
Harris v Empress Motors Ltd [1983] 3 All E.R. 561 .... 22–30, 23–15
Harris v Evans [1998] 1 W.L.R. 1285 11–20
Harris v James (1876) 45 L.J.Q.B. 545 14–25
Harris v Wyre Forest DC [1990] 1 A.C. 831 11–19